Adventures are waiting
for you, GO!!!

Cindy

Adventures of Lion, the Mule

Cindy Stuart

Adventures of Lion, the Mule

Now to him who is able to accomplish far more than all we ask or imagine, by the power at work within us, to Him be glory in the church and in Christ Jesus to all generations, forever and ever. Amen.

Ephesians 3:20

Lion, a mule, worked hard serving people. He packed their goods over the mountain trails year after year.

No complaining, only grateful for a
at and a smile from the people he
erved.

Lion faithfully stood each morning waiting to receive the load for the day, and off he went to do the job. It wasn't a glamorous job, but this was what God created him to do, so he always picked up one hoof after the other and walked his path to please his Master.

Sometimes, on freezing nights, standing there waiting for the warmth of the sun to rise, God would send angels to keep him warm. Lion was always grateful.

Somedays, his Master would pack Lion's load a little heavier to make up for one of his fellow pack mules that had a hurt leg or aching back. Lion usually didn't question his Master no matter how heavy the load was. He just kept his eyes on the trail ahead, one hoof in front of the other, and soon the day was over.

Lion faced wolves circling him on the trail, trying to frighten him to jump into the canyon below.

Not Lion, his eyes ahead, one hoof in front of the other steady and sure. He always delivered his load safe and secure.

As time went on, Lion's strength began to fade. After thirty years of heavy loads on narrow rocky paths his body became tired, yet his heart was strong.

Lion's Master could see his favored partner was ready to spend his last days in a pasture of green grass.

When Lion arrived at Lone Eagle Ranch the owners found a special place in their hearts for him.

One of the workers, Bradley, was especially drawn to this unlikely friend.

Lion's ribs showed and his coat was dull. Bradley began to brush him.

Lion could feel this love releaving years of carrying heavy loads. Lion was grateful for Bradley's kindness.

One thing Lion didn't like was being alone, so he didn't eat.

But then he met Big Henry, a
white-faced steer. A what?!
A steer.

Lion thought this isn't my herd. But as he had learned, his Master always knew best. So he reached out to become a friend.

Lion's new friends put a smile in his heart, his Master always provided for him.

On the warm sunny days, Lion would watch Bradley and Big Henry play kick ball. This was a strange sight for Lion to see, yet it brought a smile to Lion's heart.

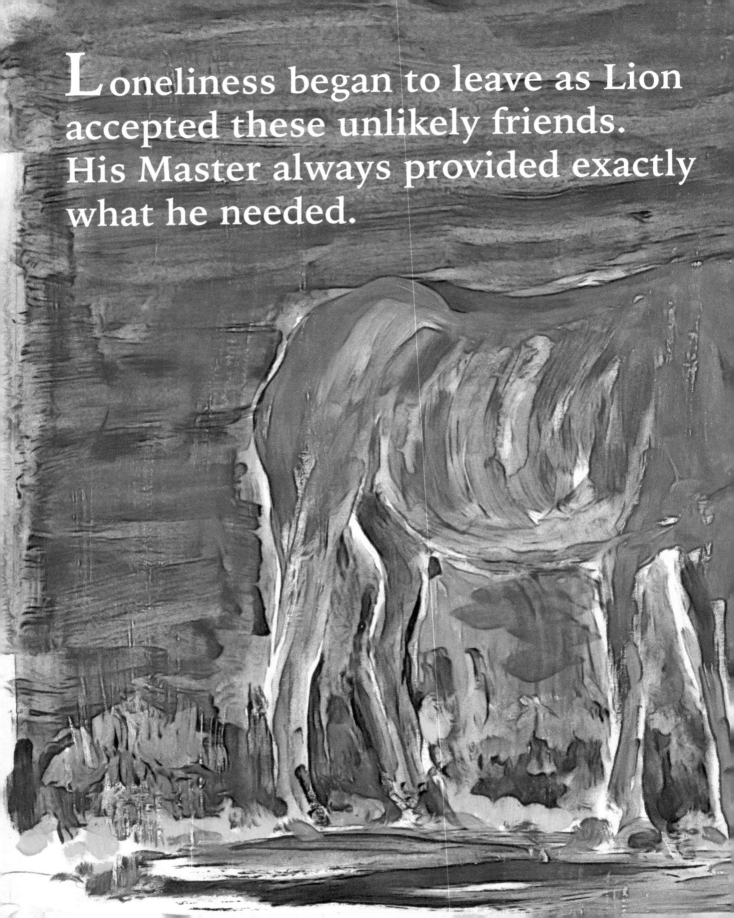

Loneliness began to leave as Lion accepted these unlikely friends. His Master always provided exactly what he needed.

As summer passed, the cold, wet winter came. Big Henry noticed his friend was weak.

Lion was laying down on a cold rainy day. Big Henry went over and stood up to watch over Lion, giving him a lick to show respect and concern.

Big Henry knew Lion would not be with him in the days to come. He could feel it was time for Lion to go to heaven.

Now, Big Henry was alone but seemed to be okay.

Bradley visited
him and brought
marshmallows.
Big Henry liked
this treat because
it reminded him of
the clouds in Heaven
where his friend Lion
is waiting for him.

Meet Bradley, Lion the Mule, and Henry, the white-faced steer, who inspired this book.

Special Dedication

I dedicate this book to my grandson, Bradley, whose heart uniquely loves animals. Without my grandson's encouragement, "Grandma, you can do it," this book would not be in your hands.

To my Granddaughter Amber, she told me, Be you, Be True, Be Bold. These words held me up with the courage to write this book.

I thank Bruce and Sue Boblet, the Lone Eagle Ranch owners, for opening up their hearts to so many people experiencing good old-fashioned life on a ranch.

To Lisa Stirrett: Her generous heart. She opened her studio as a meeting place so I could collaborate with my publisher and artist. Like a true artist, her touch of wisdom here and there added to the color of this book.

To Susan Sullivan: I am grateful to have Susan as the artist for this book. She has a love for animals and a gift of putting colors together that makes this book alive for the children as they look and listen, also for the readers as well, it will touch your heart.

To Hunter Martin: a life gone too soon. He showed me the deeper meaning of love. A love not earned but of total surrender, so others could learn how to love. I knew I was in His presence when Hunter smiled.

Meet the Author

Cindy Stuart has lived all her life in the beautiful Northwest. She spent many summers at her Uncle Tommy's dairy farm, bringing home as many kittens as she could hide under her coat. She learned the value of hard work and good homemade ice cream.

She is a mother of four children, ten grandchildren, and one great-granddaughter. Each challenged her and strengthened her to keep going no matter what life threw at her. She volunteered her way into a job in Special Education, unaware of how the job would change her life. She learned to love with no ceiling or walls.

In 1997 her Aunt Mary sent a blank journal, with an inscription, "I know you will have a lot of good feelings to put in this book." Twenty-four years later, she still journals and always will. Yet, Aunt Mary saw something in her she did not know she had.

Her faith in God is an ever-present inspiration. She never intended to write this book and even tried to get others to write it. But then, on the morning of January 1, 2021, she sat down to journal, and this book was like a download from heaven. It all just happened, and she knew it should be published.

She has her tennis shoes on, ready to come and read to you. But, the best is yet to come.

She would love to have your feedback.
Send a message Cindystu51@gmail.com

Meet the Artist

Susan Sullivan started drawing horses as soon as she could hold a crayon. While her favorite subject has always been horses, she is adept at portraying farm and country life from cowboys to old barns. Her work has an authenticity gained from varied experience such as galloping and conditioning polo horses, moving cattle on large ranches in the Pacific Northwest, and training horses.

The artist has worked in a variety of mediums from pencils to jewelry to sculptor's wax. The act of creating is challenging and fun whether she is painting wildlife or classic cowboy life on vintage saws or if she is painting elegant, horse portraits on canvas.

Susan has exhibited and sold her works at major horse shows, trail rides, national Western Art shows, mule days shows and Rodeos. Her work has been sold to Germany, Australia, and various provinces in Canada.

Send a message: sullivan_artist@hotmail.com

CPSIA information can be obtained
at www.ICGtesting.com
Printed in the USA
BVHW060725101121
620397BV00002B/24